T0346280

Tropical Island

ACTIVITY BOOK

Contents

Welcome

1  **Trace. Then read and match.**

Hello, I'm Lindy.

Hello, I'm Pippin.

Hello, I'm Joe.

Hello, I'm Emily.

 1
 2
 3
 4

2 **Write. Then draw and say.**

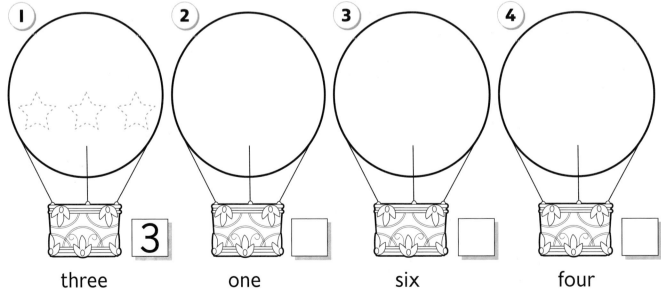

1 3 three

2 one

3 six

4 four

 **Trace. Then find and colour.**

1 = red   2 = yellow   3 = green
4 = blue   5 = pink   6 = purple

1 My toys

1

Match. Then trace and say.

1. It's a <u>boat</u>.

It's a <u>car</u>.

It's a <u>ball</u>.

It's a <u>train</u>.

It's a <u>doll</u>.

It's a <u>bike</u>.

2 **1:12** 🖊️ Listen and ✔ or ✗. Then colour.

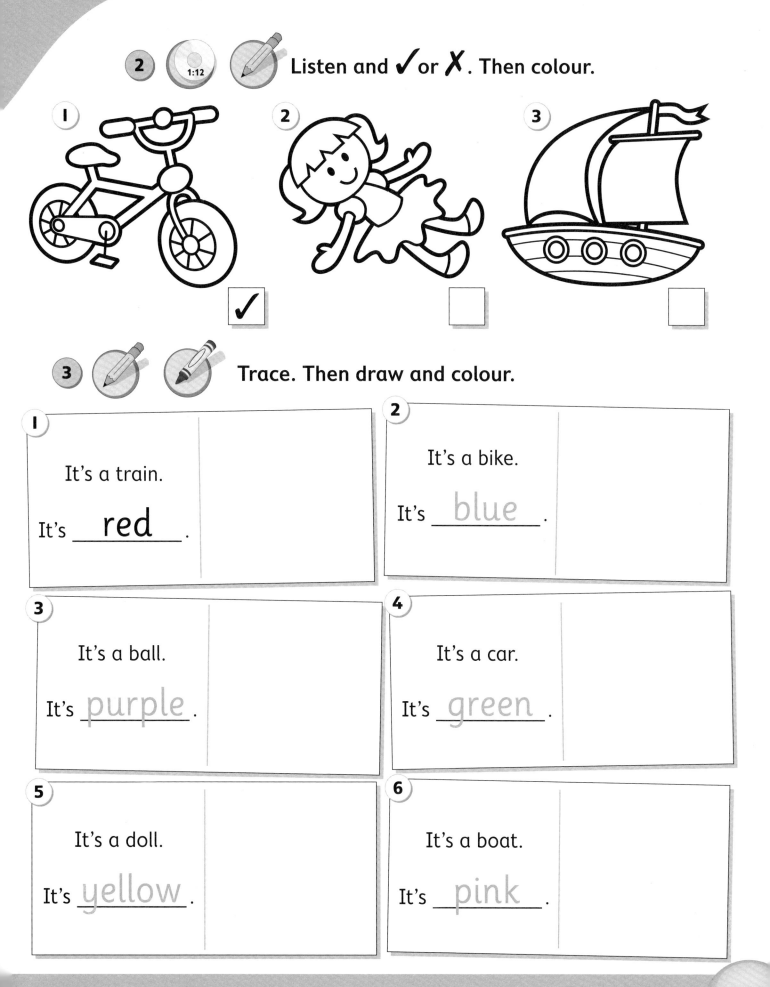

1

2 ✔

3

3 🖊️ ✏️ Trace. Then draw and colour.

1 It's a train.

It's ___red___.

2 It's a bike.

It's ___blue___.

3 It's a ball.

It's ___purple___.

4 It's a car.

It's ___green___.

5 It's a doll.

It's ___yellow___.

6 It's a boat.

It's ___pink___.

4 Match and say.

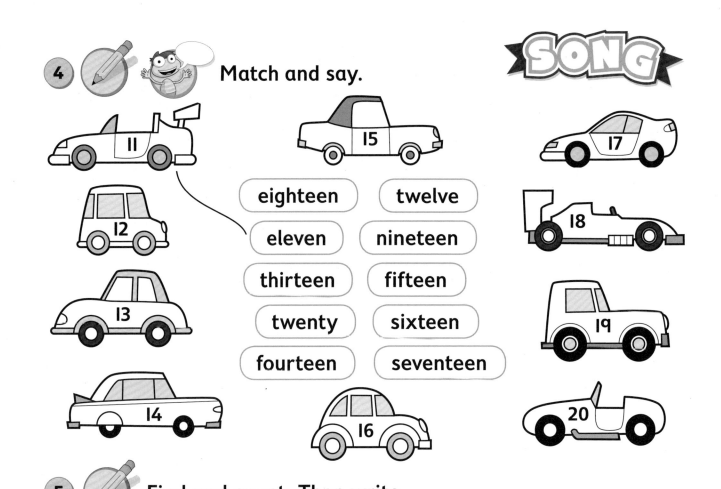

eighteen   twelve

eleven   nineteen

thirteen   fifteen

twenty   sixteen

fourteen   seventeen

5 Find and count. Then write.

How many balls? _____ balls.

6   Listen and number.
Then trace and match.

frog [1]

box [ ]

doll [ ]

pen [ ]

hen [ ]

ten [ ]

7  Find and colour.

e = red

o = orange

 **8** Write.

doll   ball   car   train   boat

What's this?

1
It's a ___**ball**___.

2
It's a _____.

3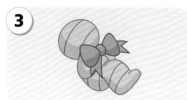
It's a _____.

4
It's a _____.

5
It's a _____.

9  Draw. Then number and say.

1

2

It's a doll. It's Princess Emily.

It's Pippin. He's a parrot. ☐

Listen and write.

1   = __4__ dolls

2   = _____ trains

3   = _____ bike

4    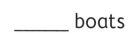 = _____ boats

11  **Write. Then say.**

1

2 ✚ 12 ▭ _____

3 ▬ 7 ▭ _____

12   **Read and colour.**

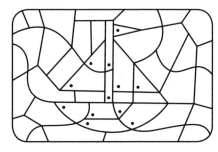

1 It's a car.
It's blue.

2 It's a boat.
It's yellow.

3 It's a doll.
It's purple.

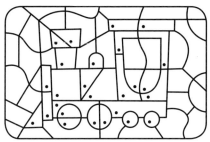

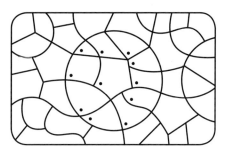

4 It's a bike.
It's green.

5 It's a train.
It's orange.

6 It's a ball.
It's pink.

13 **Find and stick. Then colour.**

LOOK!

1 Ten dolls.
2 It's a train.
3 It's blue.

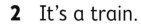

2 My family

1 Match. Then trace and say.

This is my family.

mum   granny   sister

dad   grandad   brother

Read. Then look and write.

house   garden

Where's my mum?

In the _____ garden _____ .

Where's my brother?

In the _____ .

Where's my sister?

In the _____ .

Where's my dad?

In the _____ .

Where's my grandad?

In the _____ .

Where's my granny?

In the _____ .

3 🔊 1:31 ✏️ Listen and match.

SONG

1 mum

2 dad

3 sister

4 brother

5 granny

6 grandad

Where's my … ?

living room   kitchen
~~bedroom~~   bathroom

4 ✏️ Now circle and write. Then say.

1 Where's my sister?   He's / (She's) in the ___bedroom___ .

2 Where's my brother?   He's / She's in the _____ .

3 Where's my granny?   He's / She's in the _____ .

4 Where's my grandad?   He's / She's in the _____ .

5 1:33 🖉 Listen and match. Then trace.

SOUNDS FUN!

1
2
3
4

5

mum   dad
bus   van
bug   map

6

6 1:34 🖉 Listen and circle the odd one out.

1
2
3
4

7   Listen and number.

 **2**

 my mum ☐

 my dad ☐

 my sister 1

 my brother ☐

 my grandad ☐

 my granny ☐

8 Write. Then match and say.

brother ~~dad~~ grandad

 1 My ___dad___ .

Who's missing?

 2 My _____ .

 3 My _____ .

9  Number. Then write and say.

| mum | dad | granny | grandad | brother | sister | ~~baby~~ |

___baby___

_____ _____

_____ _____   _____ _____

10  Read and ✔. Then trace and say.

He's ___young___.   She's ___old___.

11 Read and look. Then write.

1 Where's my _____**mum**_____? She's in the bedroom.

2 Where's my _____? He's in the kitchen.

3 Where's my _____? She's in the living room.

4 Where's my _____? He's in the bathroom.

~~mum~~
granny
dad
brother

  12 Find and stick.

 **LOOK!**

1 Where's my mum?
2 She's in the kitchen.
3 He's in the house.

3 My body

1  **Match. Then trace and say.**

arms [7]

legs [ ]

hands [ ]

feet [ ]

fingers [ ]

toes [ ]

head [ ]

Look and write. Then trace and say.

hands   body   toes   ~~arms~~   legs   feet

1

Wave your _arms_ .

2

Clap your _____ .

3

Move your _____ .

4

Shake your _____ .

5

Stamp your _____ .

6

Touch your _____ .

3   **Read and find. Then colour.**

I've got three arms and three hands. I've got nine fingers. I've got two legs, four feet and eight toes. I'm green.

4 **Listen and write. Then draw.**

1 I've got ___four___ arms.

2 I've got _____ legs.

3 I've got _____ hands.

4 I've got _____ feet.

5 I've got _____ fingers.

6 I've got _____ toes.

7 I'm _____ .

5 **1:51** ✏ Listen and match.
Then trace.

SOUNDS FUN!

1

2

3   green

feet   fish

three   sister

green   pink

4   pink

5   3

6

6 ✏ **1:52** Match. Then listen and check.

fish   hand   leg   three

pen   six   feet   van

7  **Listen and match.**

Jump! Jump!

Hello! My name's Frank.

I'm hot!

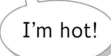

1

2

3

8  **Read and number.**

1 Jump.
2 Stamp your feet.
3 Touch your toes.
4 Shake your body.
5 Clap your hands.

q  **Look and write. Then say.**

dance   jump   swim

1

2

3

_____   _____   _____

10 **Read and find. Then number.**

| 5 | Wave your arms. |
| Jump. |
| Clap your hands. |
| Touch your toes. |
| Dance. |

 **Look and write. Then say.**

six hands eight ~~body~~ two toes ~~one~~ arms

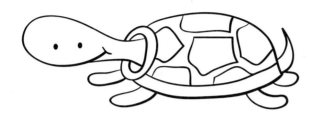 

1 I've got __one body__ . **2** I've got _____ .

3 I've got _____ . **4** I've got _____ .

 Find and stick.

1 I've got ten fingers.
2 Clap your hands.
3 Jump.

4 My face

1  Look and write. Then say.

~~face~~   eyes   ears   nose   mouth   hair

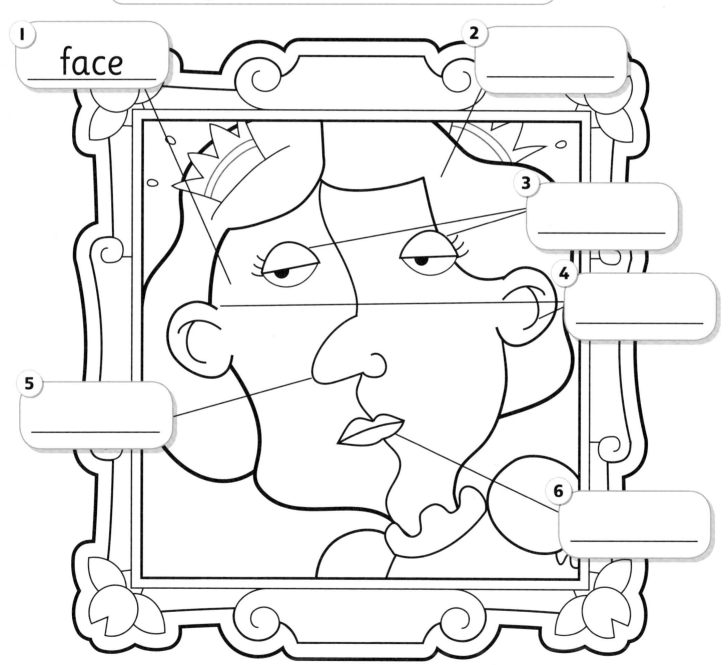

1 ___face___

2 _____

3 _____

4 _____

5 _____

6 _____

2 📖 ✏️ **Read and match.**

1

2

small eyes   short hair
big eyes   a big nose
long hair   a small nose

3

4

5

6

3 📖 ✏️ **Read. Then look and write.**

1

2

I've got big eyes.   `2`

I've got a big nose. ☐

I've got small eyes. ☐

I've got short hair. ☐

I've got long hair.   ☐

I've got a big mouth. ☐

4   **Listen and colour.**

5 **Read. Then look and circle.**

1 She's got big eyes. (Yes) / No

2 He's got long hair. Yes / No

3 She's got a small mouth. Yes / No

4 He's got a small nose. Yes / No

5 She's got short hair. Yes / No

6 **2:10** 🖊 Listen and number.
Then trace.

clothes ☐

nose ☐

old ☐

baby ☐

play ☐ I

shapes ☐

7 🖍 Find and colour. Then say.

o = red

a = blue

   Draw and say.

  **Read and match.**

He's got a big nose.
She's got big eyes.
He's got a small mouth.
She's got long hair.

10 Count and write. Then say.

11 Listen. Then look and circle.

1 (Yes) / No   **2** Yes / No   **3** Yes / No   **4** Yes / No

12 Draw. Then write and say.

It's a _____ .

13   **Read. Then look and write.**

| long | big | small | ~~short~~ | small |

1

He's got ___short___ hair.

She's got _____ eyes.

He's got a _____ mouth.

2

She's got _____ hair.

He's got _____ ears.

14 **Find and stick.**

LOOK!

1 He's got a small nose.
2 She's got long hair.
3 It's a circle.

5 Animals

1  **What's missing? Write. Then draw and say.**

hen   horse   cow   ~~goat~~   duck   sheep

1 _goat_

2 _____

3 _____

4 _____

5 _____

6 _____

 **Colour. Then say.**

1.

2.

3.

4.

 **Look at Activity 2. Then read and write *Yes* or *No*.**

1.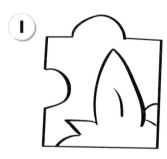

2.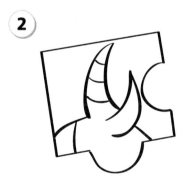

3.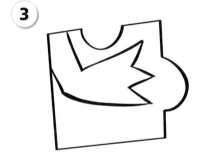

Is it a horse? __Yes__   Is it a cow? _____   Is it a sheep? _____

4.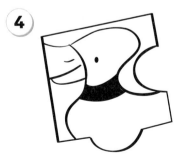

5.

Is it a duck? _____   Is it a goat? _____

Look and write.
Then listen and colour.

cat	frog	duck	horse

1  **2** **3** **4**

___horse___   _____   _____   _____

5   **Read. Then look and write.**

(dog)   (hen)   (sheep)

1 It's got two legs.   It's a ___hen___ .

2 It's got big ears.   It's a _____ .

3 It's got white legs.   It's a _____ .

4 It's got a black face.   It's a _____ .

6 2:26 ✏️ Listen and match. Then trace.

horse   cow

1 crown   **2** four   **3** house   **4** torch

7 2:27 ✏️ Listen and circle two words.

horse

cow

1 eye （torch） arm （four）   **2** jump   brown   mouth   orange

goat

duck

3 nose   three   clothes   dad   **4** crown   mum   bug   head

8 2:29 Listen and write. Then draw.

duck   sheep   cow   parrot

1  It's a ___duck___ !

2 It's a _____ !

3 It's a _____ !

4 It's a _____ !

9 Read and match.

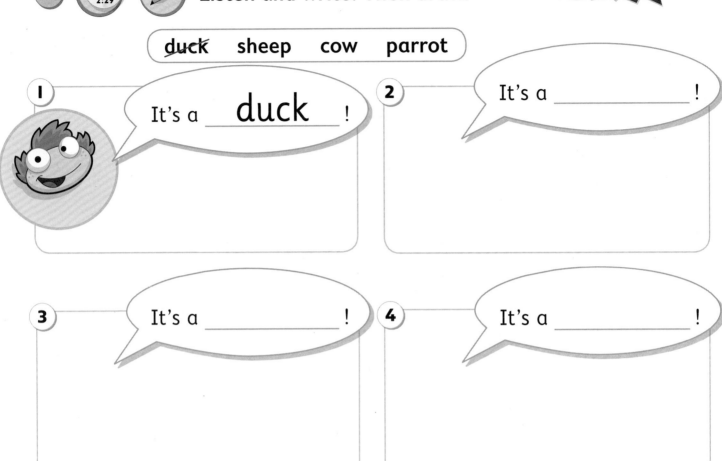

1 It's got two legs. It's thin.

2 It's got wings. It's got big eyes.

3 It's got four legs. It's got a black face.

4 It's got four legs. It's fat.

10  Match. Then trace and say.

1

2

3

bat

cow

horse

owl

duck

fox

 4

 5

 6

11  Draw animals from Activity 10. Then listen and check.

 day

 night

12  **Look and write. Then say.**

| horse | big | small | four | two | duck |

1 It's ___**big**___ .

2 It's got _____ legs.

3 It's a _____ .

4 It's _____ .

5 It's got _____ legs.

6 It's a _____ .

13 **Find and stick. Then colour.**

1 It's fat.
2 It's got four legs.
3 Is it a cow?

6 Food

 Look and write. Then draw and say.

pizza   banana   chicken   apple   fish   egg   salad   rice

1 _egg_

2 _____

3 _____

4 _____

5 _____

6 _____

7 _____

8 _____

 **2** **Look and write. Then say.**

chicken   eggs   bananas   apples

1 I like ___chicken___ .   **2** I like _____ .

3 I like _____ .   **4** I like _____ .

   3 **Read and look. Then circle and say.**

I like …

   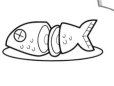

chicken   apples   salad   pizza   bananas   rice   fish   eggs

4   Listen and draw.

1

2

3

4

5

6

5   Find and write. Then say.

1

I like ...

2

I don't like ...

salad   pizza   eggs   ~~fish~~

1 I like ___**fish**___ and _____ .

2 I don't like _____ or _____ .

6  Find and colour.

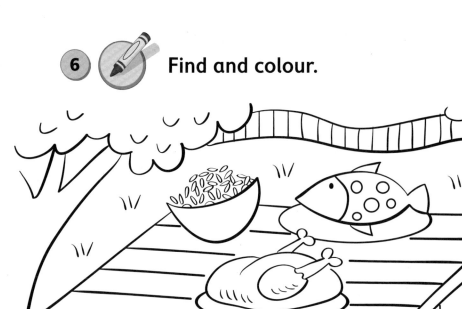

bike rice mice

7 2:44 Listen and match. Then say.

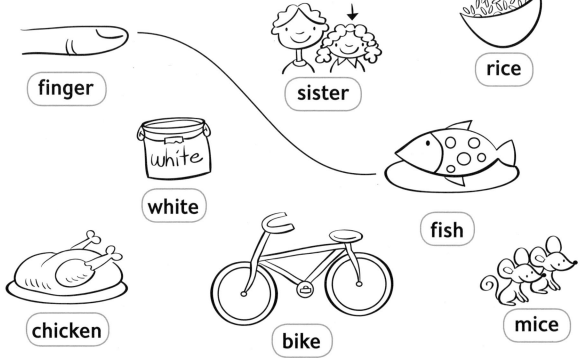

finger

sister

rice

white

fish

chicken

bike

mice

 **8** Read and circle. Then say.

1 I like / (don't like) apples.

2 I like / don't like fish.

3 I like / don't like pizza.

4 I like / don't like cake.

9   Read and circle *Yes* or *No*.

I like Pippin.

1 I like Pippin.   (Yes)/ No

2 I don't like parrots.   Yes / No

3 Pippin is my friend.   Yes / No

4 It's my birthday.   Yes / No

   Read. Then look and number.

1 I like toast and bananas for breakfast.

2 I like cereal for breakfast.

3 I like pizza for lunch.

4 I like fish and salad for dinner.

  1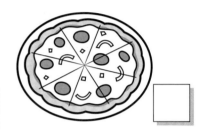

 Find and circle.

c	h	e	e	s	e	f	a	c
r	p	i	z	z	a	i	p	h
i	t	o	a	s	t	s	p	i
c	e	r	e	a	l	h	l	c
e	d	s	a	l	a	d	e	k
g	f	b	a	n	a	n	a	e
g	r	b	r	e	a	d	h	n

**Listen and circle.
Then write.**

I like ...
cereal
(chicken)
cheese
fish
apples
salad

I don't like ...
toast
pizza
bread
bananas
eggs
rice

1 I like __chicken__

and _____ .

2 I don't like _____

or _____ .

13 **Find and stick.**

1 I like apples.
2 I don't like pizza.
3 I like toast for breakfast.

7 Clothes

 **1** Find and colour. Then write.

△ = orange ○ = blue □ = red ☆ = pink ● = brown ■ = green

dress   shoe   ~~T-shirt~~   trousers   socks   skirt

1 an orange ___T-shirt___

2 blue _____

3 a green _____

4 red _____

5 a brown _____

6 a pink _____

2 Read and number. Then colour.

1. I'm wearing yellow socks.

2. I'm wearing a red dress.

3. I'm wearing a black skirt.

4. I'm wearing purple trousers.

3 Read and colour. Then look and write.

blue

red

brown

green

yellow

orange

1 I'm wearing **brown** shoes and a _____ skirt.

2 I'm wearing a _____ T-shirt and _____ trousers.

3 I'm wearing a _____ dress and _____ socks.

Lesson 2 47

4   **Write. Then listen and check.**

shoes   school   ~~pyjamas~~   T-shirt   jumper   bed   boots   pyjamas

1

Take off your **pyjamas** .

2

Put on your _____ .

3

Put on your _____ .

4

It's time for _____ .

5

Take off your _____ .

6

Take off your _____ .

7

Put on your _____ .

8

It's time for _____ .

5   **Listen and match.
Then trace.**

1

2

3

nurse

purple

bird

T-shirt

skirt

4

5
purple

6   **Match. Then listen and say.**

bird   horse   mice   train

baby   skirt   torch   bike

7  **Read. Then match and say.**

I'm wearing pyjamas.

I'm wearing a dress.

I'm wearing a jumper.

1

2

3

Lindy

Emily

Joe

8  **Draw.**

9   **Write. Then say.**

| firefighter | police officer | ~~nurse~~ | chef |

1  **2**  **3**  **4**

I'm a **nurse** .   I'm a _____ .

　　　I'm a _____ .   I'm a _____ .

10   **Read. Then find and number.**

I'm wearing black trousers and black shoes. I'm wearing a hat. **4**

I'm wearing a dress, a hat and black shoes. ☐

I'm wearing a long coat and boots. I'm wearing a big hat. ☐

I'm wearing a T-shirt and trousers. I'm wearing white shoes and a big hat. ☐

11 **Read. Then look and write.**

trousers   skirt   jumper   socks   boots   shoes   hat   T-shirt   dress

1

I'm wearing

a __dress__ ,

a _____

and _____ .

2

I'm wearing

a _____ ,

a _____

and _____ .

3

I'm wearing

_____ ,

a _____

and _____ .

  12 **Find and stick.**

LOOK!

1 I'm wearing black boots.
2 Put on your shoes.
3 Take off your hat.

8 Weather

 Look and read. Then circle and write.

cloudy   sunny   rainy   snowy   windy

Is it rainy?

Yes / (No)

It's _____sunny_____ .

Is it windy?

Yes / No

It's _____ .

Is it sunny?

Yes / No

It's _____ .

Is it cloudy?

Yes / No

It's _____ .

Is it snowy?

Yes / No

It's _____ .

2 **Ask and answer. Write *Yes* or *No*.**

Do you like rainy days?

No.

Do you like ...	Me	My friend, _____
... rainy days?		
... sunny days?		
... cloudy days?		
... snowy days?		
... windy days?		

3   **What do you like? Draw, write and say.**

sunny   cloudy   snowy   windy   rainy

1 I like _____ days.   **2** I don't like _____ days.

 **Look. Then read and number.**

Picture 1

Picture 2

1 It's cloudy. ☐ **|**

2 I've got a train. ☐

3 I'm wearing a dress. ☐

4 I've got a doll. ☐

5 It's sunny. ☐

6 I'm wearing a T-shirt and trousers. ☐

7 I like pizza. ☐

8 I like chicken. ☐

9 Look at my dog. It's big. ☐

10 I'm wearing boots. ☐

5 ✏️ Find and colour.

scooter   blue   boot   shoe   two   moose

6 🔊 3:28 ✏️ Listen and circle the odd one out.

1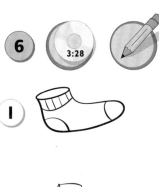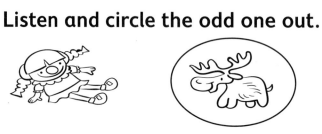

2

3

4

7 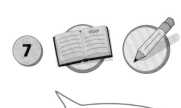 **Read and match.**

But Pippin's my friend.

Wow! You're the Princess!

My new friends. Joe and Lindy.

1

2

3

8 **Draw and write. Then say.**

Now I've got **four** friends!

Hello, I'm _____.

9   **Look and write.**
Then listen and check.

| Saturday | Tuesday | Thursday | Wednesday |

Monday | _____

Tuesday | Friday

_____ | _____

| Sunday

10 **Read. Then look and ✓ or ✗.**

| Monday | Tuesday | Wednesday | Thursday | Friday | Saturday | Sunday |

1 It's Tuesday. It's windy. ✓

2 It's Thursday. It's rainy. ☐

3 It's Sunday. It's cloudy. ☐

4 It's Saturday. It's rainy. ☐

5 It's Monday. It's snowy. ☐

6 It's Friday. It's sunny. ☐

  Read. Then find and write.

windy	sunny	cloudy	snowy

1  **2**  **3**  **4**

He's in the garden.
It's __windy__ . **3**

She's got a bike.
It's _____ . ☐

I'm wearing big boots!
It's _____ . ☐

I'm wearing a jumper.
It's _____ . ☐

  Find and stick.

1 It's windy.
2 I like snowy days.
3 Do you like rainy days?

Picture dictionary

Numbers

1 one	2 two	3 three	4 four	5 five	6 six	7 seven	8 eight	9 nine	10 ten

11 eleven   12 twelve   13 thirteen   14 fourteen   15 fifteen

16 sixteen   17 seventeen   18 eighteen   19 nineteen   20 twenty

My toys

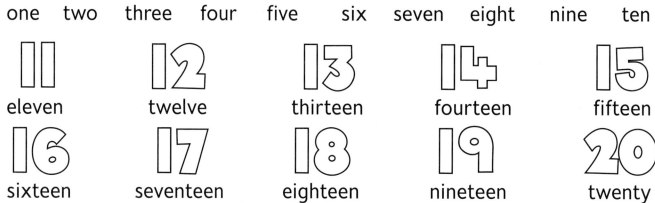

ball   doll   bike   boat   car   train

My home

mum   dad   sister brother   granny grandad   house   garden

My body

head   arms   hands   fingers   legs   feet   toes   body

My face

| face | eyes | ears | nose | mouth | hair |

Animals

| cow | horse | goat | sheep | duck | hen | cat | dog |

Food

apple   fish   banana   pizza   chicken   rice   egg   bread   cheese   salad

Clothes

| T-shirt | skirt | socks | shoes | trousers | dress |

Weather

| rainy | sunny | cloudy | snowy | windy |

61

Christmas

1 Match. Then trace and say.

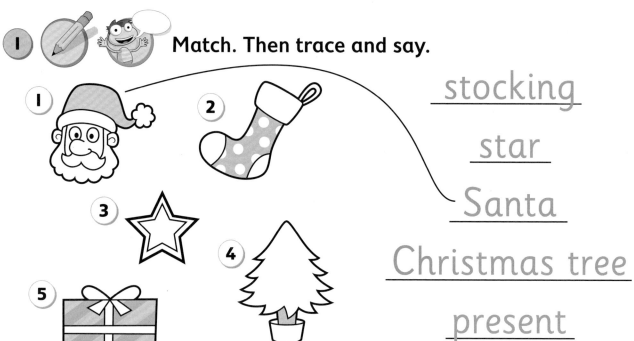

1 stocking

2 star

3 Santa

4 Christmas tree

5 present

2 Look and colour.

1 = red   2 = green   3 = black   4 = blue   5 = yellow

Valentine's Day

1  Write the words.

balloon flowers heart
card ~~chocolates~~

1

2

3

4

5

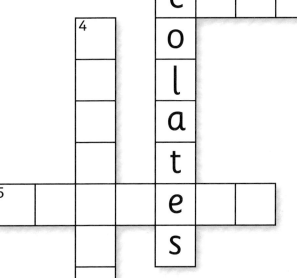

2  Draw a present for a friend.

Here's a present

for _____.

Easter

1 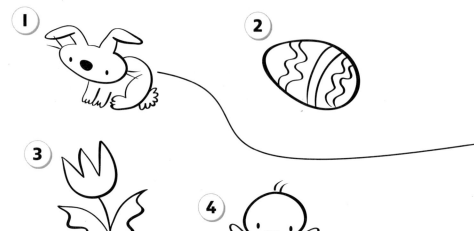 Match. Then trace and say.

1

2

3

4

egg

chick

rabbit

flower

2 Read. Then count and write.

1 How many chicks? ⬛ 5

2 How many eggs? ☐

3 How many flowers? ☐

4 How many rabbits? ☐